Animal Peculiarity Volume 3 Part 3

By T.P Just

~~~

Copyright © 2010 by Terence Just. All rights reserved.

Get All The Books In The Series:

Animal Peculiarity Volume 1 Part [1-8]
Animal Peculiarity Volume 2 Part [1-8]
Animal Peculiarity Volume 3 Part [1-8]
Just Enterprises

I0436209

Table of Contents

1. Introduction

The unique characteristics of animals is a miscellany of facts, genuine or supposed, gleamed from earlier and contemporary Greek writers (No Latin writer is once named) and to a limited extent from his own observation to illustrate the habits of the animal world.

We are of course prepared to encounter much that modern science rejects, but the general tone with its search after the picturesque, the startling, even the miraculous, would justify us in ranking Aelian with the paradoxical, rather than with the sober exponents of natural history.

Mythology, mariners' yarns, vulgar superstitions, the ascertained facts of nature — all serve to adorn a tale and, on occasion, to point a moral. His religion is the popular stoicism of the age. Aleian repeatedly affirms his belief in the gods and in divine providence; the wisdom and beneficence of Nature are held up to veneration; the folly and selfishness of man are contrasted with the untaught virtues of the animal world. Some animals, to be sure, have their failings, but he chooses rather to dwell upon their good qualities, devotion, courage, self-sacrifice, gratitude. Again, animals are guided by reason, and from them we may learn contentment, control of the passions, and calm in the face of death.

His primary object is to entertain and while so doing to convey instruction in the most agreeable form. Some might find fault with his random and piece-meal handling of his theme-of which he is well aware, and he defends himself with the plea that a frequent change of topic helps to maintain the reader's interest and saves him from boredom.

As to the permanent value of his work he has no misgivings and since we have been informed that his writings were much admired, we may assume that they appealed to cultivated circles in a way that the voluminous and possibly arid compilations of grammarians did not.

Now I am well aware of the labour that others have expended on this subject, yet I have collected all the materials that I could; I have clothed them in untechnical language, and am persuaded that my achievement is a treasure far from negligible. So if anyone considers them profitable, let him make use of them; anyone who does not consider them so may give them to his father to keep and attend to.

2. The Cow and Aphrodite

There is a district in Egypt called Chusae (it is reckoned as belonging to the province of Hermopolis, and though small in extent it possesses charm) and there they worship Aphrodite under the title of Urania (heavenly).

They also pay homage to a cow, and this, they say, is the reason: they believe that cows are related to this goddess, because the cow feels a strong incitement to love and is more passion- ate than the bull, At any rate at the sound of his bellow the cow becomes excited and inflamed with a burning desire to couple.

And those who are expert in these matters maintain that a cow hears a bull as much as thirty stades away when it is bellowing as a signal to love and mate. And in Egypt sculptors and painters represent Isis herself with the horns of a cow.

3. The Ass and the Antelope, hated in Egypt

The people of Busiris and of Abydos in Egypt and of Lycopolis dislike the blare of a trumpet on the ground that it resembles the braying of an Ass. And those who attend to the cult of Serapis also hate the Ass.

Now Ochus the Persian knowing this slew Apis and deified the Ass from a wish to pain the Egyptians to the utmost. And so he too paid a penalty, which all applauded, to the Sacred Bull, no less than Cambyses who was the first that dared commit this sacrilege.

And the same ministers of the aforesaid Zeus (i.e. Serapis) detest the antelope as well, and for this reason: the Egyptians maintain that it voids its excrement after turning its back towards the rising sun.

And the followers of Pythagoras also say this touching the Ass, that it alone among animals was not born in tune, and that this accounts for its being completely deaf to the sound of the lyre. Some moreover say that it was beloved of Typho. And in addition to the foregoing charges they would blame the Ass for this also: fertility in all kinds is respected, but this animal is by nature opposed to it. At any rate it is not easy to recall any account of a she-ass giving birth to twins.

4. The Ibis

Here is another peculiarity of the Ibis which I have learnt from Egyptian narratives. When it buries its neck and head beneath its breast-feathers, it imitates the shape of the heart. Of its special hostility to creatures injurious to man and to crops I think I have already spoken earlier on.

The birds couple with their mouth and beget offspring in that way. And the Egyptians say, though I for one 'am not easily persuaded, yet they say that those who see to the embalming of animals and who are experts at it, agree that the entrails of the Ibis measure ninety six cubits.

I have heard further that its stride when walking measures a cubit. And when the moon is in eclipse it closes its eyes until the goddess shines out again. It is said to be beloved of Hermes the father of speech because its appearance resembles the nature of speech: thus, the black wing-feathers might be compared to speech suppressed and turned inwards, the white to speech brought out, now audible, the servant and the messenger of what is within, so to say.

Now I have already mentioned that the bird lives to a very great age. And, Apion states that it is immortal and adduces the priests of Hermopolis as witnesses to prove it. Yet even he considers that this is very far from the truth, and to me it would seem to be an absolute falsehood.

The Ibis is a very hot-blooded creature, at any rate it is an exceedingly voracious and foul feeder if it really does eat snakes and scorpions. And yet some things it digests without difficulty, while others it easily expels in its excrement.

And very rarely would one see a sick Ibis, yet it thrusts its beak down in every place, caring nothing for any filth and treading upon it in the hope of tracking down something even there.

And yet when it turns to rest it first of all washes itself and purges. It makes its nest in the top of date-palms in order to escape the cats, for this animal cannot easily clamber and crawl up a date- palm as it is constantly impeded and thrown off by the protuberances on the stem.

5. The Baboon

It occurs to me now to mention the following additional facts relating to Baboons. If a Baboon finds some edible object with a shell on it (I mean almonds, acorns, nuts) it strips the shell off and cleans it out, after first breaking it most intelligently, and it knows that the contents are good to eat but that the outside is to be thrown away.

And it will drink wine, and if boiled or cooked meat is served to it, it will eat its fill; and it likes well-seasoned food, but food boiled without any care it dislikes.

If it wears clothes, it is careful of them; and it does everything else that I have described above. If you put it while still tiny to a woman's breast, it will suck the milk like a baby.

6. The 'Thermuthis' asp

They say that the asp to which the Egyptians have given the name Thermuthis is sacred, and the people of the country worship it, and bind it, as though it was a royal headdress, about the statues of Isis.

And they deny that it was born to destroy or injure man, but when they maintain that it does not touch virtuous people but kills evildoers they are romancing.

If however this is so, then Justice would value this asp beyond all things, for taking vengeance on her behalf and for its piercing sight. Others add that Isis sends it against the worst transgressors.

And the Egyptians assert that the Thermuthis alone among asps is immortal, and they reckon sixteen different species and varieties.

And in their temples, as they say, they build dens and burrows like shrines in every corner and make homes for the Thermuthes, and at intervals they provide them with calves' fat to eat.

7. The Linnet

Those who know about birds say that the bird Acanthus "derives its name from the acanthus which provides it with food. And its voice is wonderfully harmonious and tuneful. And Aristotle says that if one pours the blood of the Acanthus and of the Aegithus, as it is called, into the same vessel and wants to mix them, the two kinds will not mix and unite into a single compound. They say that the Acanthus is sacred to the gods who escort and conduct men on a journey.

The Turtle-dove
I have stated earlier on that the Turtle-dove is continent and does not, from a desire for some strange and alien bed; consort with any other mate than the one it originally joined.

And I learn from those who enquire minutely into such matters that white Turtle-doves are often to be seen. These, they say, are sacred to Aphrodite and Demeter, while the other kind is sacred to the Fates and the Erinyes

.

The Partridge

When Partridges are sitting on their eggs they screen them with branches and other thick leafage in order to keep out the dews and showers and every kind of damp. For if their eggs get soaked, unless the mother bird is quickly on the spot to warm them again, they become sterile.

Partridges lay as many as fifteen eggs at a sitting.

Theophrastus says somewhere that a double heart is to be seen in the Partridges of Paphlagonia. Other sources tell us that the Partridge is the darling of the daughter of Zeus and Leto.

The Swan

I have indeed spoken earlier on about Swans, but I shall now relate what I did not mention then. Aristotle says that a flock of Swans was once seen in the Libyan Sea, and that a melody was heard proceeding from them as from a choir singing in unison; and very sweet it was, although mournful and calculated to move the hearers to pity.

And some of the birds, he says, when the music was ended were seen to have died. It seems that the Swan is devoted to springs and pools and meres and to all spots where waters meet and abound. At any rate that is where those learned in these things say that the bird meditates its music.

8. The Owl, an evil omen

If an Owl accompanies and stays beside a man who has set out on some business, they say it is no good omen. Witness the case of Pyrrhus of Epirus who set out for Argos by night: this bird met him as he was on horseback and bearing his lance erect.

Whereupon it perched upon the lance and would not leave him: it was no safe lancer-guard that the bird I named afforded him. At any rate Pyrrhus reached Argos and met the most inglorious death in the world.

That is why I think that Homer knowing full well that the Owl was nowhere a favorable omen, says that Athena sent a heron from the rivers to the comrades of Diomedes when they went off to spy upon the Trojans' camp — a heron, not an owl, even though it appears to be her favourite. And that the country about Troy is moist and well-watered Homer can bear witness in the lines that precede the Battle at the Wall.

Octopus and Crayfish

The Octopus is the terror of the Crayfish. At any rate if they chance to be caught in one and the same net, the Crayfish dies on the spot.

Black fish

There is a river at Thurii called the Lusias, of which the water is of the purest and is absolutely transparent in its flow, and yet it produces fish of a deep black hue.

The 'Ampelus' leopard

They say that there is a leopard called the Ampelus, like the plant (i.e. grape-vine), and that its nature is peculiar compared with other leopards; and I have heard that it has no tail. If it is seen by women it afflicts them with an unexpected ailment.

The Horned Ass of Seythia

In Scythia there are Asses with horns, and these horns hold water from the river of Arcadia known as the Styx; all other vessels the water cuts through, even though they be made of iron.

Now one of these horns, they say, was brought by Sopater to Alexander of Macedon, and I learn that he in his admiration set up the horn as a votive offering to the Pythian god at Delphi, with this inscription beneath it:

'In thine honour, O God of Healing, Alexander of Macedon set up this horn from a Scythian ass, a marvelous piece, which was not subdued by the untainted stream of the Lusean Styx but with-stood, the strength of its water.' It was Demeter who caused this water to well up in the neighborhood of Pheneus, and the reason for it I have stated elsewhere.

9. Eupolis and his dog

Augeas of Eleusis gave Eupolis, the writer of comedies, a
hound of fine appearance, a Molossian, which Eupolis named
after the donor. Now Augeas the hound, pampered in its
feeding and influenced by long association with its master,
came to love him.

On one occasion a young fellow-slave of the name of Ephialtes
stole some plays of Eupolis, and the theft did not pass
unnoticed, for the hound saw him, fell upon him, and, biting
him mercilessly, killed him.

Some time afterwards Eupolis ended his days in- Aegina and
was buried there, and the hound, howling and lamenting after
the manner of dogs, let himself pine away through grief and
starvation and, disgusted with life, died soon after on the
grave of the master that had fed it. And in memory of the sad
event the place is named Hound's Dirge.

10. The 'Laertes' ant and wasp

They say that there is a species of deadly Ant, and that it goes by the name of Laertes. The name has also been applied to certain kinds of Wasp. This is what Telephus the grammarian from Pergamum in Mysia says.

Fish in the Nile mud

All through the hottest summer the Nile in flood gives the fields of Egypt the appearance of a calm stretch of open sea, and over what was till then ploughland there the Egyptians fish and sail in boats manufactured against that season and against this visitation by the river.

Later the river retreats and returns to within its naturally proper limits, while the fish bereft of their sire and abandoned by the flood water are left behind, nurtured in the thick slime to provide a meal for the farmers. This then, though, the expression is somewhat violent, is the Egyptian fish-harvest.

11. The Cicada: various kinds

There are, it seems, many species of Cicada, and those who are skilled in these matters enumerate them and report their names.

Thus, the Ashen one is so called from its colour; whence the Membrax got its name I do not know; and Chirper, it appears, is the name for a Cicada; and I have heard tell of the Long-tail and the Shriller and the Prickly one.

Well, these are all the kinds of Cicada of which I remember having heard the names, but if anyone has go to know more than those that I have mentioned, he must tell them.

12. The Dog Honoured In Egypt

Here are further facts relating to Dogs which I have heard. Puppies are born blind, and when they emerge from their dam's womb they cannot see. For the first fortnight they are afflicted in this way that is for as many nights as the moon does not appear, but after that the Dog has the sharpest sight of any animal.

And it is held in honour by the Egyptians, for they have named a district after it, and they assert that the reason for this is twofold: first, when Isis was seeking everywhere for Osiris, Dogs led the way and tried both to help her to trace his son and also to keep off the wild beasts.

And the second reason is this, that at the same time that the Dog—star rises (the story goes that it was the dog of Orion), the Nile also in a sense rises, coming up to water the land of Egypt, and pours over the plough- lands. And so the Egyptians pay honour to the Dog for bringing and summoning this fertilizing water.

13. The Oxyrhynchus fish

There is a fish that goes by the name of Oxyrhynchus and it appears to derive its name from its face and from the shape of it. The Nile breeds the aforesaid fish; and after it too a district is named, where, I believe, this same fish is held in veneration. Should the inhabitants catch a fish on a hook they will never eat it for fear lest the aforesaid fish, which they regard as sacred and to be worshipped, may have chanced to impale itself on the hook.

And whenever fish are netted, they search the nets in case this famous fish has fallen in without their noticing it.

And they would rather catch nothing at all than have the largest catch which included this fish. And the people who live round about maintain that it was born from the wounds of Osiris. They identify Osiris with the Nile.

14. The Ichneumon

The Ichneumon is both male and female in the same individual, partaking of both sexes, and Nature has enabled each single same animal both to procreate and to give birth. Those that are worsted in a fight are degraded into the less honored class, for the victors mount the vanquished and inseminate them.

And the latter carry with them as prize of their defeat endurance of birth-pangs and motherhood for fatherhood. The Ichneumon is most hateful to man's deadliest enemies, the asp and the crocodile:

I have earlier on described how they war with each other. Ichneumons are said to be sacred to Leto and the Goddesses of Birth, and the people of Heracleopolis worship them, so they say.

15. The story of Pindus and a Serpent

To Lycaon King of Emathia was born a son of the name of Macedon, after whom the country has thenceforward been called, no longer preserving its ancient name. Now his son was a vigorous youth of remarkable beauty and his name was Pindus.

Other sons he had besides, but they were foolish in spirit and not robust of body, and so in course of time growing jealous of the valour and the general good fortune of their brother, they slew him; but it was to their own undoing, and they paid the penalty as was right.

For Pindus realising that his brothers were plotting against him, left his father's kingdom and lived in the country. And besides being vigorous in- other respects he was also a great hunter. And on one occasion he was pursuing some fawns, and they fled as fast as their legs could carry them, while he rode at full speed in pursuit, leaving his fellow hunts-men far behind.

But the fawns entered a hollow and very deep ravine, escaped out of their pursuer's sight, and disappeared. Accordingly Pindus leapt from his horse and fastened it by the rein to one of the trees hard by and was just about to investigate the ravine and to search for the fawns, when he heard a voice which said ' Touch not the fawns!

And so after looking all round and seeing nothing, he was in fear of the voice, thinking that it proceeded: from some mightier agency; and then he departed taking his horse with him. But on the following day he came unaccompanied, but remembering the voice that had fallen on his ears and being afraid, he did-not enter the ravine.

And while was taking council with himself and was perplexed as to who it was that the day before had checked his pursuit of the quarry, and while he was looking about, as was natural, for shepherds on the hills or other hunters, he beheld a monstrous serpent trailing most of its body behind but with the neck, which was small compared with the rest of the body, held aloft.

(Neck and head together exceeded in size that of a full-grown man.) The sight filled him with terror. Pindus however did not take to flight, but pulled himself together and by his adroitness tricked the serpent, for he brought forward the birds which he happened to have caught and offered them as friendly gifts and as a ransom for his own life.

And the serpent mollified presumably and bewitched, as you might say, by the gifts, departed. This pleased the youth and thereafter, being a good man, he used to bring payment for the saving of his life to the serpent, giving freely the first fruits of the chase, whether beast or bird from the hills.

And this bestowal of gifts had the most fruitful results for Pindus, and his fortune began to prosper and grew every day more impressive, for whether it was beasts of the forest or whether it was birds, with all of them his hunting was successful.

Accordingly he enjoyed abundance; moreover his fame spread abroad, of how he fearlessly attacked and captured wild beasts. His figure was tall and such as to cause, astonishment by reason of the bulk of his body and of his splendid condition also.

And it was clear that his beauty inflamed and kindled the hearts of all women with desire for him: all who were widowed would throng his doors like people crazed, while those who were married to husbands and whom custom confined indoors were enslaved by the fame of Pindus's beauty and would rather have been his wife than become goddesses.

As to the men, most of them admired and loved him; only his brothers hated him. And once when he was hunting by himself they lay in wait for him, and the hunting- ground was near a river, and the three set upon him as he had none to help him and smote him with their swords. Whereupon he cried aloud. His cry was heard by his companion the serpent. (This creature is keen of hearing and has very sharp eyes.) And so it emerged from its lair and coiling round the miscreants killed them by choking them to death. But the snake continued to mount guard until the youth's relations, who were anxious for him, arrived and found him lying dead. But though they made lamentation for him they did not dare to attend to the dead body for fear of its guardian. The serpent however realising by some mysterious instinct that it was keeping them away, departed at a very leisurely pace, leaving Pindus to receive the last kind service from his kin.

And so he was buried with great pomp, and the river which was close by the scene of murder was called Pindus after the dead man and the tomb over him. It is then a characteristic of animals to render thanks to their benefactors, as I have stated earlier on, and especially on this occasion.

16. Clarus free from noxious creatures

Particularly in Clarus do the inhabitants and all Greeks pay honour to the son of Zeus and Leto. And so the land there is untrodden by poisonous creatures and is also highly obnoxious to them.

The god wills it so, and the creatures in any case dread him, since the god can not only save life but is also the begetter of Asclepius, man's saviour and champion against diseases.

Moreover Nicander also bears witness to what I say, and his words are:

No viper, nor harmful spiders, nor deep- wounding scorpion dwell in the groves of Clarus, for Apollo veiled its deep grotto with ash-trees and purged its grassy floor of noxious creatures

The worship of Aphrodite at Eryx

I have heard it said that in Eryx, where of course the famous temple of Aphrodite is (the pigeons there and their peculiarities I mentioned earlier on), there is a store of gold, an immense store of silver, necklaces, and finger-rings of great price; and that dread of the goddess renders them safe from robbers and untouched; and that men in ancient times always regarded the aforesaid goddess and her treasures with veneration and awe.

But I learn that Hamilcar the Carthaginian looted these objects, melted down the silver, and gold, and then distributed an infamous largesse to his troops. And for these deeds he suffered the most painful and grievous torments and was punished with crucifixion, while all his accomplices and partners in that unholy sacrilege died violent and terrible deaths.

And his native land which till then was so prosperous and which was reputed enviable above most lands, after these sacred objects had been imported, was reduced to slavery. But impressive though these facts are they have no bearing on my present object, but what is relevant to this discourse shall now be told.

On every day throughout the whole year the people of Eryx and strangers too sacrifice to the goddess. And the largest of the altars is in the open air, and upon it many sacrifices are offered, and all day long and into the night the fire is kept burning.

The dawn begins to brighten, and still the altar shows no trace of embers, no ashes, no fragments of half-burnt logs, but is covered with dew and fresh grass which comes up again every night. And the sacrificial victims from every herd come up and stand beside the altar of their own accord; it is the goddess in the first place that leads them on, and in the second place it is the ability to pay, and the wish, on the part of the sacrificer.

At any rate should you desire to sacrifice a sheep, lo and behold, there is a sheep standing at the altar, and you must begin the ceremonial washing. But if you are a man of substance and wish to sacrifice one cow or even more than one, then the herdsman will not mulct you by charging too much, nor will you disappoint him, for the goddess sees that the sale-prices are just, and if you pay fairly you will win her favour.

If however you want to buy at a cheaper rate than is proper, you will pay down your money in vain--the animal departs and you are unable to sacrifice. So much then for this peculiarity of animals at Eryx in addition to those which I have mentioned earlier on.

17. Swans and the worship of Apollo

The race of the Hyperborean's and the honours there paid to Apollo are sung of by poets and are celebrated by historians, among whom is Hecataeus, not of Miletus but of Abdera. The many other matters of importance which he narrates I think there is no need for me to bring in now, and in fact I shall postpone the full recital to some other occasion, when it will be pleasanter for me and more convenient for my hearers. The only facts which this narrative invites me to relate are as follows. This god has as priests the sons of Boreas and Chione, three in number, brothers by birth, and six cubits in height.

So when at the customary time they perform the established ritual of the aforesaid god there swoop down from What are 'called the Rhipaean mountains Swans in clouds, past numbering, and after they have circled round the temple as though they were purifying it by their flight, they descend into the precinct of the temple, an area of immense size and of surpassing beauty.

Now whenever the singers sing their hymns to the god and the harpers accompany the chorus with their harmonious music, thereupon the Swans also with one accord join in the chant and never once do they sing a discordant note or out of tune, but as though they had been given the key by the conductor they chant in unison with the natives who are skilled in the sacred melodies.

Then when the hymn is finished the aforesaid winged choristers, so to call them, after their customary service in honour of the god and after singing and celebrating his praises all through the day, depart.

18. Serpents sacred to Apollo in Epirus

The people of Epirus and all strangers sojourning there, beside any other sacrifice to Apollo, on one day in the year hold their chief festival in his honour with solemnity and great pomp. There is groves dedicated to the god, and round about it a precinct, and in the enclosure are Serpents, and these self-same Serpents are the pets of the god.

Now the priestess, who is a virgin, enters unaccompanied, bringing food for the Serpents. And the people of Epirus maintain that the Serpents are sprung from the Python at Delphi. If, as the priestess approaches, they look graciously upon her and take the food with eagerness, it is agreed that they are indicating a year of prosperity and of freedom from sickness.

If however they scare her and refuse the pleasant food she offers, then the Serpents are foretelling the reverse of the above, and that is what the people of Epirus expect.

Dogs sacred to Hephaestus at Etna

At Etna in Sicily honour is paid to a temple of Hephaestus, and there are precincts, sacred trees and a fire that is never extinguished, never sleeps.

And about the temple and the grove there are sacred Hounds which greet and fawn upon such as pass into the temple and the grove with honest hearts in seemly fashion as is their duty, as though the animals had a kindness for them and presumably recognised them.

If however a man has his hands stained with crime, they bite and tear him, whereas those who only come from the bed of debauchery they simply chase away.

The worship of Demeter at Hermlone

The people of Hermione worship Demeter and sacrifice to her in splendid and impressive style; and they call her festival the 'Festival of the Earth.' At any rate I have heard that the largest cattle allow themselves to be led from the herd by the priestess to the altar of Demeter and be sacrificed. And Aristocles bears witness to my statement when he says somewhere.

Demeter, goddess of abundance, thou dost manifest thyself both to the people of Sicily and to the sons of Erechtheus, but this among the dwellers in Hermione is judged a mighty feat: the bull of surpassing size from a herd, which not even ten men can master, this bull an aged woman, coming by herself, leads by the ear alone to this altar, and he follows as a child after its mother. Thine, even thine, Demeter, is the power. Show us thy favour and grant that every farm in Hermione may thrive exceedingly.

Dogs sacred to Athena in Daunia

In the country of the Daunii there is a temple to Athena of Ilium which is celebrated. And they say that the Hounds that are kept there fawn upon any Greeks that arrive but bark at foreigners.

A refuge for hunted animals in Arcadia

And in Arcadian territory there is a shrine of Pan; Aule is the name of the place. Now any animals that take refuge there the god respects as suppliants and protects in complete safety. For wolves in pursuit are afraid to enter it and are checked at the mere sight of the place of refuge. So there is private property for these animals too to enable them to survive.

19. A refuge for hunted Deer in Cyprus

On Curias when the Deer (of which there are a great number and many hunters keen in pursuit of them) take refuge in the temple of Apollo there (the precinct is of very wide extent), the hounds bay at them but do not dare to approach.
But the Deer in a body graze undeterred and without fear and by some mysterious instinct trust to the god for their safety.

20. Flies avoid the festival of Apollo

I have mentioned somewhere earlier on how on the occasion of the national assembly at Olympia the flies absent themselves of their own free will and, so to speak, depart along with the women to the opposite bank of the Alpheus. And in the island of Leucas there is a high promontory on which a temple of Apollo has been built, and worshippers style him Apollo of Actium.

Now when the festival is about to be held there in which they make the Leap in honour of the god, men sacrifice an ox to the flies, and when the latter have sated themselves with the blood they disappear.

Yes, but they are bribed to depart, whereas the flies at Pisa need no bribe. So the latter are superior because they do what is required out of reverence for the god and not for a reward.

Hunting on Ichara

Icarus is an island and lies in the Red Sea. Now there is a temple of Artemis there and quantities of wild goats and plump gazelles and hares also. If a man asks leave of the goddess to take them and then starts to hunt whatever is allowed, he does not fail in his object but succeeds and is glad of her gift. But should he fail to ask, he takes nothing and is punished in a Way that others describe.

21. Apis, the sacred bull of the Egyptians

And now, when I have mentioned the swans from the Rhipaean Mountains in the country of the Hyperboreans on account of their daily and assiduous service of the son of Zeus and Leto, shall I refrain from telling of the special characteristics of the sacred Bull which the Egyptians deify? How then could I avoid being censured by history and by Nature, who made and gave this gift also to man? But (no one shall accuse me of negligence on this point ? and I will describe also, as is reasonable, this system of religion. Among the Egyptians Apis is believed to be the god whose presence is most manifest. He is born of a cow on which a flash of light from heaven has Fallen and caused his engendering. The Greeks call him Epaphus and trace his descent from his mother the Argive Io, daughter of Inachus.

The Egyptians however reject the story as false, and appeal to time as their witness, for they maintain that Epaphus was born late down the ages, whereas the first Apis visited mankind many, many thousands of years earlier, adduce evidence and tokens of this; but the Egyptians do not acknowledge them, for they assert that there are nine-and — twenty marks clearly to be seen on this sacred bull.

But what these marks are, and how they are distributed over the body of the animal, and in what fashion the bull is, as it were, adorned with them, you may learn from another source. And the Egyptians are able to explain which of the stars each mark symbolises.

And they say further that the marks indicate when the Nile will rise and the shape of the universe. But you will also see a mark (so the Egyptians assert) which suggests that darkness is older than light.

And another mark explains the shape of the crescent moon to him who understands; there are besides, other mysterious signs of different import which to the eyes of the profane and those uninstructed in divine history are hard to interpret.

And whenever the report gets abroad which tells the Egyptians that the god has been born, some of the sacred scribes to whom there has been handed down from father to son the science whereby they verify these marks, come to the spot where the calf has been born to the heifer beloved of god, and in accordance with the immemorial precepts of Hermes erect a house where the calf will live at any rate for the time being; it faces the rising sun and is quite large enough to take in the nurses of the calf, for it is essential that the calf should be at the udder for four months.

And when it has been weaned, then at the rising of the new moon the sacred scribes and priests go out to meet it and moreover year by year make ready a sacred vessel for this god and transport him on board to Memphis, where he finds abodes after his heart and delightful spots to linger in and places where he may amuse himself, where he may run and roll in the dust and exercise himself, and the homes of beautiful cows, and a well and a spring that yield water for drinking, for his ministers and priests say that it is not good for him always to drink of the Nile.

Moreover he is said to grow fat on this sweet water which helps to build up a mass of flesh. As for the processions which they hold and the sacred offices which they perform when the Egyptians celebrate the revelation of the new god, the dances which they execute, the feasts and the assemblies which they organize, and how every town and village is filled with joy — all this would make a long story.

But the man in whose herd this divine animal was born is counted fortunate and is so, and the Egyptians regard him with admiration.

Apis, it seems, is in effect a good prophet: he to be sure never sets girls or elderly women on tripods, never fills them with some sanctified draught, but a man prays to this god, and children without, who are playing and dancing to the music of pipes, become inspired and proclaim in time with the music the actual response of the god, so that what they say is more true than what occurred by the Sagras.

The Egyptians liken Apis to Horus Whom they believe to be the prime cause of the fertility of their crops and of every good season. That is how they come to reason about his varied colouring, seeing in it a hidden symbolical reference to the variety of the crops.

And there is a story of the priests not known to all, that Menis the King of Egypt, thinking of some living animal that he might worship, elected a bull, believing it to be the finest of all animals, and at any rate following Homer in his judgment on these matters, so they say. For Homer too in his Iliad says. 'Even as a bull standeth out far foremost in the herd, for he is conspicuous amid the pasturing kine.'

But the facts which Egyptian writers on zoology distort into legends about this animal are not to my taste.

Mneuis, the sacred bull of the Egyptians

'Nay, but change the theme', as the phrase might go, and sing not of the Horse nor yet of the ambush within, but of the bull Mneuis. And he, say the Egyptians, is sacred to the Sun, whereas Apis, they say, is dedicated to the Moon.

And according to the Egyptians he also bears a special mark to show that he is no counterfeit, no bastard, but beloved of the aforesaid god. On these topics another shall speak, but what I wish to tell is the Egyptians' account of the test and the proof to which they put this bull to see whether he is of superior birth or not.

And King Bocchoris

Bocchoris the King of Egypt acquired — I do not know how — a false reputation and an fictitious renown and appeared to be just in his judgments and to have his heart set on righteousness. But by nature, it seems, he was the reverse. Most of his actions I pass over at present, but this is how, from a. desire to cause pain to the people of Egypt, he treated Mneuis. He set a wild bull against him. So Mneuis began to bellow and the newcomer bellowed in answer.

And then the stranger rushed forward in anger intending to fall upon the bull beloved of the god, but tripped and falling against the stem of a persea-tree, broke his horn, whereupon Mneuis wounded him in the flank and killed him. Boccharis was put to shame and the Egyptians loathed him.

But if anyone considers it highly undignified to drop from natural history into legend, he is a fool. For I am stating what the practice is with these bulls, and what then occurred, and what I hear Egyptians say . . .a lie to them is an abomination.

22. The Dolphin

The Dolphins' love of music and their eager pursuit of song have been noised abroad and spread to many quarters, and others have told of their friendliness to man, and we ourselves have discoursed upon it earlier on, I think.

But here I shall do well to speak of their intelligence. At any rate when ever a Dolphin is enclosed in a net he keeps quiet to begin with and does not think of escaping, but feasts upon the fish that have been caught with him and, as though invited to a banquet, takes his fill of them.

But as soon as he realises, while being drawn along, that he is nearing the shore, he thereupon bites through the net, escapes, and is free. If however he is caught, the more kindly fishermen pass a rush through his nostrils and let him go; and the Dolphin, as though he were ashamed of the evidence of his capture, never comes near a drag-net again.

23. The Elephant as nurse

I have earlier on spoken of the differences and the varieties in the character of Elephants, and I shall now tell what a good memory too this animal has, how it can remember orders and not belie the expectation and the hope of those who entrust it with whatever it may be.

For instance when Antigonus was besieging Megara a female elephant of the name of Nicaea was being kept along with one of the war-elephants. Now to this animal the wife of the keeper entrusted a baby which she happened to have borne a month before, speaking the Indian language, which Elephants understand.

And the Elephant grew fond of the child and used to look after it, and liked to have it lying near, and would glance at it when it Whimpered; and when it slept the Elephant would scare away the flies, holding in her trunk a spray from the reeds which were thrown beside her as her fodder.

And if the child was not there she would actually put her own food aside. And so the mother was obliged to give the child its fill of milk and then place it beside its guardian, otherwise Nicaea gave unmistakable signs of being annoyed and angered and even of threatening mischief.

And often, if the baby started to cry, she rocked the cradle in which it lay, comforting it as nurses are in the habit of doing by the swaying-and this, my fellow-men, was an Elephant.

An Elephant punishes adultery

I know that I have spoken appropriately of the very violent jealousy on the part of different mg animals, viz the coot, the dog, and in the third place the stork. But now I intend to speak of the anger of an Elephant over an outraged marriage.

Having detected the wife of its trainer and keeper in the very act of adultery, it drove one tusk through the woman and one through her lover and killed them both and left them lying amid the dishonored coverings on the desecrated bed, so that when the trainer came he might note their sin and recognise his avenger.

This happened in India, but the deed travelled from there to these shores, and I learn that in the reign of Titus, that good and noble man, the same thing occurred in Rome, but they add that the Elephant there killed both the offenders and covered them with a cloak which on the arrival of its keeper it threw oft and revealed the two lying side by side, while the tusk with which it had pierced them was seen to be stained with blood.

24. Safeguards and remedies for animals

Here are further peculiarities of animals. The Peacock in order to escape the influence of the evil eye seeks out a root of flax as a kind of natural amulet and carries it about packed under one wing. And it is said that if a horse suffers from retention of urine and a maiden strikes him across the face with the girdle she is wearing, he immediately stales copiously and is relieved of his pain.

And when a mare shows an altogether frenzied desire to go a horsing it is easy to arrest her, according to Aristotle if one clips the mane on her neck. For she feels shame and is no longer skittish and drops her wantonness and her constant frisking and is downcast at her disgrace. And Sophocles, you remember, in his drama of Tyro hints at this. Tyro is represented as speaking, and this is what she says

' But it is my lot to grieve for my hair, even as a filly which seized by neatherds in the stables has had the yellow harvest reaped from her neck with ruthless hand; and haled to the meadow to drink of the stream, beholds the mirrored image of her reflexion with the hair cropped beneath the shears to her dishonour. Alas! even a pitiless heart would pity her, cowering in her shame, to see how wild are her grief and her tears for her lost hair.'

Animals give warning impending disaster

When a house is on the verge of ruin the mice in it, and the martens also, forestall its collapse and emigrate. This, you know, is what they say happened at Helice, for when the people of Helice treated so impiously the Ionians who had come to them, and murdered them at their altar, then it was (in the words of Homer that 'the gods showed forth wonders among them.' For five days before Helice disappeared all the mice and martens and snakes and centipedes and beetles and every other creature of that kind in the town left in a body by the road that leads to Cerynea. And the people of Helice seeing this happening were filled with amazement, but were unable to guess the reason.

Earthquake at Alice

But after the aforesaid creatures had departed, an earthquake occurred in the night; the town collapsed; an immense wave poured over it, and Helice disappeared, while ten Lacedaemonian vessels which happened to be at anchor close by were destroyed together with the city I speak of.
Justice at the same time uses animals as her ministers to punish impious men. Witness the case of Pantacles the Lacedaemonian who, after preventing some of the artists of Dionysus who were on their way to Cythera from passing through Sparta, later, when seated upon the Ephor's throne, was torn to pieces by dogs.

Sacred Hounds in the temple of Adranus

Adranus is a town in Sicily, according to Nymphodorus, and in this town there is a temple to Adranus, a local divinity. And they say that he is there in very presence. And all that Nymphodorus tells of him besides, and how he shows himself and how kindly and favourable he is to his suppliants, we shall learn some other time.

But now I shall give the following facts. There are sacred Hounds and they are his servants and ministers; they surpass Molossians in beauty and in size as well and there are not less than a thousand of them. Now in the daytime they welcome and fawn upon visitors to the shrine and the grove, whether they be strangers or natives.

But at night they act as escorts and leaders, and with great kindness conduct those who are already drunk and staggering along the road, guiding each one to his own house, while those who indulge in tipsy frolics they punish as they deserve, for they leap upon them and rip their clothes to pieces and chasten them to that extent. But those who are bent on highway robbery they tear most savagely.

25. A Red Sea Snail

There is, it seems, a marine snail which is born in the Red Sea and of great beauty and very large. Its' shell is purple and its spiral has been decorated and made gay by Nature. You would say you were looking at a garland subtly woven of flowers of varied hue, green and golden and vermilion, the colours alternating at equal intervals.

The Dolphin in perpetual motion

Nature, they say, has caused the Dolphin to be in perpetual motion, and for the Dolphin motion ends with the end of life. At any rate when in need of sleep it rises and floats up to the surface so that its whole body is visible, and then goes to sleep.

Even the Dolphin is not unsleeping or devoid of a share of the god of sleep. At all events when it does sleep it sinks into the depths until it touches the bottom, and when it reaches it, it wakes on the impact with the floor of the sea and rises again. And again when overcome by sleep and subdued by the god, down it sinks, and again when roused by the impact as before, up it floats; and it does this time after time, being half-way between repose and activity, and yet never once does it lapse into complete immobility.

26. The 'Harper' fish

In the Red Sea there occurs a flat-fish shaped like the sole, so they say. Its scales are not very rough to the touch; its colour is golden, and from head-tip to tail it is marked with black lines. One might describe them as tense strings, which is the reason why the fish itself is called the 'Harper.
Its mouth is compressed and is a deep black and is enclosed in a saffron-coloured ring; its head is variegated, gleaming like gold and with black lines, It has fins like gold, but its tail is black except at the tip, and that is the purest white.
And other kinds of Harper are said to occur: some are purple all over, with golden lines at intervals. They have rings the colour of gillyflowers on their head: one descends from below the eyes down to the gills, another extends from behind the eyes half-way down the head, and another encircles the neck like a necklace.

27. The Leopard—fish

The Leopard—fish is native to the Red Sea, The according to those who have seen it, and in its colour and circular markings resembles the leopard of the mountains.

The 'Oxyrhynchus' fish
The Oxyrhynchus, which occurs there, has an elongated mouth, eyes like gold and white eyelids There are pale markings on its back, but the fins on either side are black, while the dorsal fins are white. Its tail is oblong in shape and its colour is green, and a streak of gold bisects it.

Ptolemy II and his Elephant
Ptolemy the Second, also called Philadelphus, was presented with a young Elephant, and it was brought up where the Greek language was used, and understood those who spoke it. Up to the time of this particular animal it was believed that Elephants only understood the language spoken by the Indians.

The Male superior to the female
It seems that among brute beasts also Nature has put the male above the female. At any rate the the male Dragon has the crest and the beard; and the Cock too has the comb and the Wattles; and the Stag has the horns, the Lion the mane, the male Cicada the voice.

Small causes of great wars
The war between the Achaeans and Trojans was caused, they say, by Helen the daughter of Zeus; the war of the Persians against the Greeks was caused by Atossa the wife of Darius who had conceived a desire to obtain Athenian women for her service; and the long war in Greece was due to the proclamation directed against the people of Megara.

The people of Magnesia and of Ephesus were roused to war by a locust; the people of Chaonia and of Moesia by a dove; and the people of Thebes in Egypt are said to have made war against the Romans because of a dog.

Victor and vanquished

There is a story that Pythochares the piper repelled an attack of wolves by playing a loud and noble strain on his pipe. And a swarm of flies drove out the people of Megara, wasps the people of Phaselis, and centipedes the people of Rhoeteum.

28. The Sheep of Pontus and of Naxos

They say that the Sheep of Pontus have no gall—bladder, whereas those on the isle of Naxos have two.

The Bee-eater
The Bee-eater appears to be more dutiful than the stork, for this reason: it does not wait for its parents to grow old before it starts to feed them, but does so directly it grows its quill-feathers.

Serapis restores a Horse's eye
Here is another characteristic of animals and a good one. The gods take thought for them, neither looking down upon them nor reckoning them of small account.

For although destitute of reasoning power, at any rate they possess understanding and knowledge proportionate to their needs. And I will explain how they are beloved of the gods, not by many examples taken from a multitude but by a sufficient number.

A cavalry officer of the name of Lenaeus owned a horse of fine appearance, very fleet of foot and of dauntless spirit; in displays it was good at running the course it had been taught; in war itself it was capable of endurance; and was quite excellent both in pursuit, when occasion arose, and in retreat, where necessity called for it.

And in consequence of all this the horse was a valued possession, and the owner was accounted most fortunate by his fellow cavalrymen. Now the horse, with the excellent qualities I have described, in consequence of a blow which it received in its right eye was incapacitated for seeing.

Accordingly Lenaeus seeing all his hopes anchored upon the condition of his noble horse (the cavalry shield covered the left eye which alone could see), went to the temple of Serapis bringing a patient of a most unusual kind,-his horse, and, as though he were pleading for a brother or a son, implored the god for the horse's sake to have com- passion on his suppliant, especially as it had done no wrong.

For men, he said, may bring misfortune upon themselves either by some impious act or some blasphemous speech. 'But what sacrilege,' he exclaimed, 'or what murder has a horse committed, and how and by what means has it blasphemed? ' And he called the god to witness that he himself had never wronged any man, and for this reason he implored the god to relieve his comrade-in-arms and friend of its blindness. And the god, although so mighty, did not neglect or scorn to heal the dumb beast, and therefore took pity both on the sick animal and on the man who besought him on its behalf, and prescribed a cure, not by fomenting the eye but by warming it with vapour baths at midday in the temple precinct.

So this was done and the eye of the horse was restored. And Lenaeus sacrificed thanks-offerings and donations for its recovery, while the horse pranced and snorted and seemed larger and more beautiful and was full of joy, and speeding to the altar moved so proudly, and as it rolled in front of the steps was seen to be giving thanks with all its might to the god who had healed it.

29. A sacred Asp and its slayer

A husbandman was digging a trench in a vine-yard in order to plant some fine, choice cutting, when he brought down his mattock upon a sacred Asp that had its lair below the soil and was far from hostile to man, and without knowing it cut the snake in half.

And as he was breaking up the soil he caught sight of the tail involved in the sand, while the severed portion from the belly upwards to the neck was still crawling and covered with gore from the cut. He was horror-struck, went out of his mind, and passed into a state of real madness of the most acute description.

By day he lost control of himself and of his reason; moreover at night he was in a state of frenzy, and would leap out of bed saying that the Asp was pursuing him, and as though he was on the point of being bitten would utter the most horrifying cries and shout for help.

He would even say that he saw the form of the snake which he had slain, angrily threatening him; at times he avowed that he had been bitten, and it was evident from his groans that he was in pain. So when his affliction had lasted for some time, his relations took him as a suppliant to the temple of Serapisand implored the god to remove and abolish the phantom of the aforesaid Asp.

Well, the god took pity on the man and cured him. But I have described how the Asp had not to wait for its revenge and a very sufficient revenge too.

A sacred Peacock

The King of Egypt was presented with a Peacock from India, the largest and most magnificent of its kind. He was unwilling to keep it along with the common flock as a household pet or for eating, but attached it to the temple of Zeus Protector of the City, judging the aforesaid bird to bean offering worthy of the god.

This bird a dissolute youth of considerable wealth longed to capture and to make a meal of, for he habitually indulged his appetite on any and every pretext, and in his extravagant gluttony and depravity he regarded variety of food and what had been acquired by dangerous means and what had been purchased at the cost of immense trouble as an accession to his pleasure.

Accordingly he offered one of the attendants on the god a substantial bribe to commit sacrilege, and promised him a further sum besides. And the man elated by a vain hope Went to the spot where he knew the bird lodged and tried to lay hands on it and bring it to his rich patron.

But the bird he did not see: what he did see was a huge asp reared up in anger against him. At first he was afraid and made off, but when the dissolute man insisted and urged him on, the attendant went to get the Peacock.

But the bird sprang up out of preach and raising itself lightly through the air on its wings, settled not upon one of the sacred trees nor upon any other lofty and high spot but upon the centre of the temple, and surveyed them with an unflinching eye as though to show that it was too clever for their designs and that it was not to be caught.

Accordingly since the attendant had accomplished nothing, the dissolute man demanded the money, which he had already given, back again; but the other refused, saying that he had carried out his orders but was unable to steal what belonged to the gods.

As was natural, a quarrel arose over the affair and presently there was shouting, and many people heard the noise. Next, the chief priest arrived and enquired what was the reason of this wrangling in the temple, and the men began to accuse one another.

And the rich man, outraged by threats, blasphemy, and abuse, took his departure, and after swallowing the bone of another bird was in pain and died in agonies, while the wicked attendant was punished by the governor of the city for sacrilege. As for the bird, it was not seen either alive or dead, but the story goes that after living for a hundred years it disappeared.

30. A victim of poisoning saved by Serapis

The following story too is like the above and concurs with it. One Cissus by name, a devoted servant of Serapis, was the victim of a plot on the part of a woman whom he had once loved and later married: he ate some eggs of a snake, which caused him pain; he was in a grievous state and in danger of death.

But he prayed to the god, who bade him buy a live Moray and thrust his hand into the creature's tank. Cissus obeyed and thrust in his hand.

And the Moray fastened on and clung to him, but when it was pulled of it pulled away the sickness from the young man at the same time. It was because this Moray was a minister of the god's healing power that the tale reached my hearing.

Cures wrought by Seraphis

And this same god in the days of Nero cured Chrysermus who was vomiting blood and already beginning to waste away, by means of a draught of bull's blood. And I mention these facts because animals are so dearly beloved by the gods that their lives are saved by them, and when the gods desire, they save others.

It was this god (Serapis) who when Basilis the Cretan fell into a wasting disease, rid him of this terrible complaint by causing him to eat the flesh of an ass. And the result was in accordance with the name of the beast, for the god said that this treatment and remedy would be of assistance to him.

On these topics enough has been said.

31. The Horse

Here are further peculiarities of animals. Mares are believed to be most suitable for drawing chariots. And I learn that trainers assert that horses delight in being washed and anointed. And Semonides in his iambics says that horses were even rubbed with perfume.

And the Persians, since the battle which Cyrus fought in Lydia, keep camels together with their horses, and attempt by so doing to rid horses of the fear which camels inspire in them.

Various genera of the animal world

Fishes that have no scales are called 'cartilaginous': for example, the moray, and the conge reel, the torpedo, the sting-ray, the horned-ray, the dog- fish; <'cetaceans'>, the dolphin, the whale, and the seal; these are the only aquatic creatures that are viviparous. 'Cephalopod mollusca' is the name given to those that have no bones: for example, the octopus, the cuttlefish, the squid, and the sea — anemone; these have no blood and no intestines.

'Crustacea,' lobsters, prawns, crabs of all kinds; these sloughs their 'old age.' 'Testacea,' oysters, purple shell- fish, whelks, trumpet-shells," sea — urchins, crayfish.

'Saw-toothed' animals are the Wolf, the dog, the lion, the leopard; these, you know, are carnivorous. Incisor-teeth in both jaws are found in man, horses, and asses and these creatures have fat. Animals whose upper and lower teeth meet evenly are the ox, the sheep, and the goat.

Animals with projecting teeth, the wild boar, the blind-rat; the elephant, I maintain, has horns, not teeth. Insects, the wasp, the bee; these are even said to have no lungs.

'Amphibians,' the hippopotamus, the otter, the beaver, the crocodile, Scaly creatures, the lizard, the salamander, the tortoise, the crocodile, the snake; and these also, with the exception of the tortoise and the crocodile, slough their 'old age.'

Animals with uncloven hoofs, the horse, the ass; cloven-hoofed animals, the ox, the stag, the goat, the sheep, the pig. Creatures with toes, men and dogs.

Web-footed and flat-nailed creatures, the swan, the goose. Creatures with crooked talons, hawks and eagles. I have mentioned elsewhere the distinguishing marks of other animals.

The Egyptian Goose

It seems that the Egyptian Goose also is devoted to its offspring and behaves as partridges do. For it also rolls on the ground in front of its young and affords its pursuer the hope of catching it; meantime the chicks make their escape. And when they are some distance away, the parent also takes wing and is off.

The Hawk

The Egyptians say that the Hawk While alive and active is beloved of the gods, and when it has departed this life and shed its body and become a disembodied spirit, it prophesies and sends dreams; and the Egyptians say that a Hawk with three legs once appeared among them, and believers accept the statement as sound.

32. Freaks of Nature

The Partridges of Paphlagonia have two hearts, according to
Theophrastus. And Theopompus says that Hares in Bisaltia
have each of them a double liver. And Apion says—unless he
is romancing--that the Stags in certain districts have four
kidneys.
And the same writer states that in the time of Atothis son of
Menis there appeared a Crane with two heads, and that there
was prosperity in Egypt; and in the reign of another King
there appeared a bird with four heads, and the Nile
overflowed as never before and the fruits were abundant and
the crops flourished marvelously. Nicocreon of Cyprus
possessed a Deer with four horns; this he gave as an offering
at Delphi and wrote beneath it:
'It was thy doing, O son of Leto, mighty archer, that Nicocreon
captured this four-horned deer.'
Moreover there were even Sheep with four horns and with
three horns in the temple of Zeus, the Guardian of the City.

And I myself have seen a sacred Ox with five feet which was an offering to this god in the great city of Alexandria, in the far-famed grove of the god, where the persea-trees close-planted afforded the loveliest shade and coolness.

And there was a Calf with the colour of wax, and it had a foot attached to its shoulder which was superfluous for walking although it was perfectly formed. True, these phenomena appear far from conformity to nature, but I have reported what I myself have seen and heard.

Get All The Books In The Series:

Animal Peculiarity Volume 1 Part [1-8]
Animal Peculiarity Volume 2 Part [1-8]
Animal Peculiarity Volume 3 Part [1-8]